Global Cities
ISTANBUL

Rob Bowden
photographs by Edward Parker

CHELSEA HOUSE
PUBLISHERS
An imprint of Infobase Publishing

Istanbul

Copyright 2007 © by Evans Brothers Limited

Chelsea House
An imprint of Infobase Publishing
132 West 31st Street
New York NY 10001

Library of Congress Cataloging-in-Publication Data
Bowden, Rob.
   Istanbul / Rob Bowden ; photographs by Edward Parker.
     p. cm. — (Global cities)
   First published by Evans Brothers Limited, London.
   Includes bibliographical references and index.
   ISBN 0-7910-8850-2 (alk. paper)
   1. Istanbul (Turkey)—Juvenile literature. 2. City and town life—Turkey—Istanbul—Juvenile literature.
I. Parker, Edward, 1961- II. Title. III. Series.
   DR723.B68 2007
   949.61'8—dc22   2006029502

Chelsea House books are available at special discounts when purchased in bulk quantities for businesses, associations, institutions, or sales promotions. Please call our Special Sales Department in New York at (212) 967-8800 or (800) 322-8755.

You can find Chelsea House on the World Wide Web at http://www.chelseahouse.com.

Printed in China.
10 9 8 7 6 5 4 3 2 1

This book is printed on acid-free paper.

Designer: Simon Walster, Big Blu Design
Maps and graphics: Martin Darlinson

All photographs are by Edward Parker (Images Everything Ltd./EASI-Images) except front cover main image, © Robert Wróblewski (Shutterstock.com); 14, by kind permission of the Trustees of the National Gallery, London/Corbis; 48, by Ken Cendeno/Corbis; and 49, by Reuters/Corbis.

First published by Evans Brothers Limited
2A Portman Mansions, Chiltern Street, London W1U 6NR, United Kingdom

Contents

Living in an urban world

Some time in 2007, history will be made. For the first time ever, the world's population will become more urban than rural. An estimated 3.3 billion people are now living in towns and cities, and for many, it's a fairly new experience. In China, for example, the number of people living in urban areas increased from 196 million in 1980 to over 536 million in 2005.

The urban challenge...

The rapid shift to a mainly urban population is being repeated around the world and provides a complex set of challenges for the 21st century. Many challenges are local: providing clean water for the people of expanding cities, for example. Other challenges are global. The spread of diseases in tightly packed cities is a problem, as is the spread of diseases between cities linked by air routes, high-speed trains, and roads. Pollution generated by urban areas is another concern, especially because urban residents tend to generate more pollution than their rural counterparts.

▼ Istanbul in relation to Turkey and its neighboring countries.

... and opportunity!

Urban centers, particularly major cities, also provide opportunities for improving life. Cities can provide efficient forms of mass transportation, such as subway or rail networks. Services such as waste collection, recycling, education, and health care can all work more efficiently in a city. Cities are centers of learning, and often the birthplace of new ideas. They provide a platform for arts and culture. As their populations become more multicultural, these become increasingly global in their nature.

▼ The European and Asian parts of Istanbul are divided by a strait called the Bosporus (in rear of image), which runs roughly north-south for some 19 miles, connecting the Black Sea to the Sea of Marmara.

A global city

Although all urban centers will share certain things in common, in some cities, the challenges and opportunities facing an urban world are particularly condensed. These are the world's global cities: they reflect the challenges of urbanization, globalization, citizenship, and sustainable development that face us all. Istanbul is one of these cities, straddling the border between Europe and Asia and grappling with the pressures to modernize while protecting its heritage. Although no longer the capital (that moved to Ankara in 1923) Istanbul remains the largest, most populous, and most culturally significant city in Turkey. This book introduces you to the city and its people, and explores what makes Istanbul a global city.

A symbolic city

"A meeting of worlds, a meeting of cultures" is how Istanbul is often described by the outside world, and in many ways this is true. It occupies a unique position, the only city in the world to be located on two continents—Asia and Europe. A strategic location, this made Istanbul one of the first truly global cities, playing a vital role in east-west trade long before cities like London or New York even existed. Today, as the forces of globalization lead to ever-greater trade and the increased mobility of people and cultures around the world, Istanbul is symbolic of these patterns. The city is grappling with how to position itself in this new world order, with influences and connections from Europe to the west, emerging Asia to the east, and the former Russian superpower to its north. Amid all of this change the city and its people must attempt to preserve their own identity and character.

▼ The center of Istanbul, showing the European side (left) and Asian side (right) flanking the Bosporus.

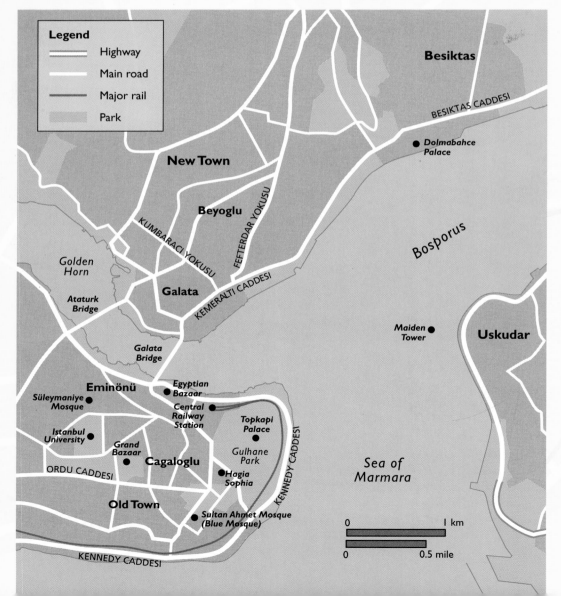

Legend

	Highway
	Main road
	Major rail
	Park

Besiktas

BESIKTAS CADDESI

Dolmabahce Palace

New Town

Beyoglu

KUMBARACI YOKUSU

FEFTERDAR YOKUSU

Bosporus

Golden Horn

Galata

KEMERALTI CADDESI

Ataturk Bridge

Maiden Tower

Uskudar

Galata Bridge

Egyptian Bazaar

Eminönü

Süleymaniye Mosque

Central Railway Station

Topkapi Palace

KENNEDY CADDESI

Istanbul University

Grand Bazaar

Cagaloglu

Gulhane Park

Sea of Marmara

ORDU CADDESI

Hagia Sophia

Old Town

Sultan Ahmet Mosque (Blue Mosque)

KENNEDY CADDESI

0	1 km
0	0.5 mile

Rising to the challenge

Rapid population growth, sprawling urbanization, and threats from pollution and natural hazards present considerable challenges to Istanbul. The city has bold visions for its future and is investing heavily in building a global city fit for the 21st century, one capable of utilizing its privileged location. Istanbul is a living testament to the history of urbanization and globalization, but its latest initiatives may be of value to other cities and help write the history of tomorrow.

▲ Modern Istanbul sprawls outward along the Bosporus and Marmara coast, creating a vast urban area that continues to expand annually.

The history of Istanbul

Istanbul—the name used by the Turks for centuries—only came to be used by non-Turks in 1930, when it was declared the official name of the city. Regardless of its name, a city has stood on this site for over 2,600 years. Throughout much of that history, Istanbul has been a coveted prize of conquest, changing hands on numerous occasions between the historic empires of Europe and Asia. The legacy of this history is found throughout the city, from its architecture and relics, to its vibrant and cosmopolitan population.

Ancient origins

The first settlements in the area of modern-day Istanbul were founded around 675 B.C.E. by the Greeks. Chalcedon is reported as the first and stood in the area that is now Kadikoy, on the Asian side of the city. According to legend, within 20 years a Greek sailor called Byzas founded a new settlement, which became known as Byzantium, in the area today occupied by Haghia Sophia, Topkapi Palace, and the Blue Mosque. Located at a strategic point on the Bosporus, with the ability to control the east-west trade routes, Byzantium soon flourished. The Persians, Athenians, Spartans, and Macedonians all vied for control of Byzantium, but it was the Romans in 196 C.E. who finally gained firm control of the city.

Roman Byzantium

By the end of the third century Byzantium had become one of the most powerful cities in the world, controlling the eastern territories of the Roman Empire. Divisions in the Roman Empire between Byzantium

▼ The Suleymaniye Mosque is regarded as the finest of the large mosques of Istanbul. It was built by Suleyman the Magnificent's architect, Sinan, between 1550 and 1557.

and Rome later led to an internal power struggle in which Constantine, the Emperor of the West (ruling from Rome) defeated Byzantium's Eastern Emperor, Licinius, in 324 C.E. This victory signaled a major shift in the history, and indeed the name, of the city. Emperor Constantine chose to move the capital of the reunified Roman Empire to Byzantium,

▶ Part of the city walls still standing in Istanbul today. The walls have been rebuilt on numerous occasions.

▲ The Valens Aqueduct dates back to the fourth century. It was built to bring water to Constantinople from as far as 125 miles away.

rebuilding it and renaming it in 330 C.E. as New Rome and Constantinople ("the City of Constantine").

Constantinople

Constantinople, as the city became known, prospered as the new capital and was rebuilt with impressive palaces and new city walls. Records of bread handouts by the Emperor suggest it had a population of at least 80,000 at this time. Besides the rebuilding, Emperor Constantine also changed the city—and indeed the entire Roman Empire—by adopting Christianity as the official religion. Churches were built across the city, which was now the distinctively Christian capital of the Roman Empire.

In the West, the Empire's grasp weakened. In the fifth century Rome itself and the western Empire were overrun by tribes from northern Europe, but in the East the Empire, with its capital Constantinople, survived for another thousand years. It became progressively Greek- rather than Latin-speaking, even though its inhabitants still called themselves Romans. This Eastern Roman Empire is now called the Byzantine Empire, but Greek-speaking Orthodox Christians in Turkey are still today referred to as Rum (which originally meant "Roman").

Threats and decline

By the 11th century, the Byzantine Empire had become much weaker. Muslim Arab armies had already conquered the Middle East (south of modern Turkey) and in 1071, a Muslim Turkish army defeated the Byzantine emperor in eastern Turkey. From then on, Muslim Turkish tribes started to settle in Anatolia (the Asian part of what is now Turkey). The Byzantine Empire shrank to areas around Constantinople and parts of the Balkan Peninsula and Anatolia. At the same time, relations deteriorated between the Orthodox Christian Church centered in Constantinople and the increasingly powerful Roman Catholic Church led by the Pope in Rome. Orthodox Christians did not accept all the papal claims to universal authority over the Church.

Faced with Turkish armies now close to Constantinople, Byzantium appealed for help from the west to drive the Turks out of Anatolia. In response, the west sent the Crusades, armies of European warriors blessed by the Pope, whose prime concern was to return Jerusalem and Palestine to Christian rule. Relations between Roman Catholic, Latin-speaking crusaders and the Greek-speaking Orthodox Christians of the Byzantine Empire were never easy. In 1204 the warriors of the Fourth Crusade stormed and ransacked Constantinople, sending much of its treasure back to Italy (mostly to Rome and Venice). They ruled the city until 1261, when it was retaken by Byzantine forces, but Byzantine Constantinople never recovered its former glory.

An Ottoman city

The Turks who had settled in Anatolia became divided into separate principalities. One group in northwestern Anatolia emerged as a new force that gradually overshadowed the other Turkish principalities. Named after their leader, Osman, they became known as Osmanli—in English "Ottomans"—and first clashed with the Byzantines in 1301. In 1394 the

▼ Portrait of Sultan Mehmet II, who conquered the city in 1453.

Ottomans laid siege to Constantinople but did not succeed in capturing the city until 1453, when it finally fell under the leadership of Sultan Mehmet II (see picture page 14).

Mehmet II—known in Turkish as Fatih Sultan Mehmet (Mehmet the Conqueror)—had a vision of Constantinople as a great cosmopolitan city where ideas from east and west could meet. He set about rebuilding the city and brought people, regardless of their religion, to repopulate it. Freedom of religion was almost unheard of in other parts of Europe at this time and indeed many people were persecuted on the basis of religion. This made Constantinople one of the most enlightened cities in the world and attracted a diversity of population that is still evident today.

The Ottoman Turks also brought Islam to Constantinople and many great churches, like Haghia Sophia, became mosques. Constantinople was again the capital of a great empire—a Muslim empire—and reached its peak under Suleyman the Magnificent (1520–66). At this time the Ottoman Turkish Empire extended east to Iraq and the Arabian Peninsula, north into southern Russia and Hungary, and west to Greece, the Balkans, and most of North Africa.

▲ The Ottoman Turks built many fine mosques in Istanbul and established Islam as the dominant religion of the city. This is Mecidiye Mosque on the shores of the Bosporus.

The end of Empire

The Ottoman Sultans remained in power in Constantinople until after the First World War (1914–18), though their power and empire were by this time much diminished. Nevertheless, they continued to develop the city as it expanded on both the European and Asian sides. A new bridge across the Golden Horn to Galata was opened in 1845 and signaled a shift in the center of the city toward what is now the commercial hub of Beyoglu and Galata. In another symbol of expansion and modernization, the Sultanate moved from Topkapi Palace in 1856 to a new western-style imperial palace, Dolmabahce, farther along the Bosporus.

In the First World War, Ottoman Turkey was allied with Germany to protect itself from perceived threats by the French, British, and Russians. Turkish forces engaged in bitter fighting against Russians in the east, and British, Australian, and New Zealand forces on the Gallipoli Peninsula, at the western end of the Sea of Marmara. The Turkish army, inspired by a young commander, Mustafa Kemal, succeeded in repelling the allies at Gallipoli, but by 1918 the German, Austrian, and Turkish alliance was defeated, and British, French, and Italian troops entered Constantinople.

▲ The Galata Bridge, when first opened in 1845 linked Galata and Eminonu, opening them up to greater commerce. The Bridge has been replaced on several occasions, most recently in 1992.

The rise of Istanbul

The defeated Ottoman Empire signed a Treaty in 1920, removing most of Turkey's territory, including areas where there was a clear Turkish majority. Together with the landing of Greek troops in western Anatolia in 1919, this provoked Turkish outrage. Mustafa Kemal used this outrage to launch a successful Turkish nationalist movement, driving Greek, Italian, and French forces out of Anatolia and signing a new treaty with the major European powers to establish the frontiers of Turkey. In 1922 the remnants of the Ottoman Empire were abolished and Turkey became a republic in 1923, with Mustafa Kemal as its first president.

Considered the savior of the Turks, Mustafa Kemal became known simply as Ataturk, meaning "father of the Turks." He embarked on a radical reform program to ensure that Turkey became a secular, western-oriented state. Seeing Constantinople as a reminder of the imperial past he moved the capital to Ankara and, in 1930, officially renamed Constantinople with its Turkish name, Istanbul. Other reforms included limiting the power of Islam to religious affairs, giving women the vote, introducing the European calendar, and adopting the Latin alphabet in place of Arabic script. Though deprived of its status as capital, Istanbul remained the cultural and economic center of Turkey, a status it maintains today. Ataturk, despite living in Ankara and traveling extensively around Turkey as president, came to Istanbul to die.

▲ Ataturk (Mustafa Kemal) formally gave Istanbul its present name in 1930, but also removed its status as the capital city upon founding the Turkish Republic in 1923.

A new direction?

Istanbul may seem to be a city lost in time, but this is far from the truth. Istanbul is a thriving global city, key to its nation and of growing stature in the broader region. Its status as a divide between Europe and Asia is still strong and remains for many its defining feature, but with Turkey seeking membership of the European Union (EU), this could change as Istanbul becomes Europe's first global mega city.

The people of Istanbul

In 2006 Istanbul had an official population of around 10 million, but other estimates place it as high as 14 million. Whatever the actual figure, Istanbul is certainly the most populous city in Europe, with only Moscow and Paris coming close. The majority of Istanbul's people are Turks, but there are also people of Kurdish origin from the southeastern regions of Turkey, and Albanians, Greeks, Jews, and Armenians. Many Turks came as refugees from the Balkan countries, which belonged to the Ottoman Empire. More recent arrivals include Russians, Ukrainians, Moldavians, Azeris, Iranians, Iraqis, Somalis, Chinese, and Koreans.

Population boom

When Ataturk ordered the first census of Istanbul following the establishment of the Turkish Republic in 1923, it returned a 1924 population of around 1.2 million. By 1950, the population had declined a little to around a million, but it has grown consistently ever since, reaching 8.8 million by 2000. This phenomenal growth is partly explained by an increase in the administrative boundaries of the city in 1984, when the city area expanded fourfold to take in 25 new municipalities. Even allowing for this expansion, Istanbul's population more than doubled between 1984 and the end of the century. Growth remains significant today, though it is slowing from the annual average rate of 3.6 percent between 1975–2000 to an expected average of 1.6 percent per year for the period 2000–2015. From such a high base population this means Istanbul's population will still grow by around 200,000 people a year (some place estimates closer to 500,000) for the foreseeable future.

◀ Istanbul has a very youthful population so even if new migration stopped, the city would still grow as its young marry and begin families of their own.

Coping with population growth

Providing housing, employment, and essential services (transportation, water, waste collection, and so on) for any city is a major challenge. For Istanbul these challenges have been amplified by the sheer speed of growth. In response, the city and its people have adopted their own coping mechanisms, such as the *dolmus* transportation system (see page 43), which provides low cost informal transportation, and the diverse informal economy (see page 34), which provides employment opportunities and vital services to the less affluent.

One visible coping strategy is Istanbul's *gecekondu*, a local word meaning "houses built by night." As the name implies, *gecekondu* consist of informal housing that often begins as hurriedly constructed homes made of locally available materials. Over time the *gecekondu* are improved and

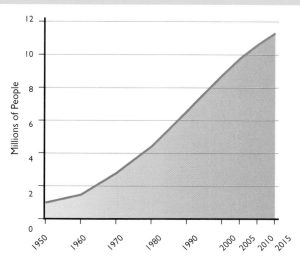

▲ Istanbul's population growth 1950–2015.

developed, but many still remain unofficial developments built on illegally occupied public land. Beyond the old city center and business district, *gecekondu* form the majority of Istanbul's suburbs. They are estimated to compose 65 percent of all buildings in the city and to house over half the population.

▲ Every day, buses and trains bring new migrants and their belongings into Istanbul. The city struggles to provide for this continual influx of people.

19

Turkish majority

Turks dominate the population of Istanbul, accounting for 75–80 percent of the total. Almost all Turks are Muslims and Istanbul is accordingly a city in which Muslims are predominant. It boasts some of the world's finest mosques (there are more than 2,500 in the city), several of which are today major tourist attractions as well as important places of worship). Islam in Istanbul (and Turkey generally) coexists alongside other religions with little tension. Turkey is a secular state, so the strict codes of Islamic dress enforced in some Islamic states do not apply (it is illegal to wear headscarves in schools and universities). But many Turks are very strict Muslims, and

▼ Hallmarks of Islamic dress such as women's headscarves are a more common sight in Uskudar on the Asian side of the Bosporus.

there can be strong social pressure on women from family members and the community to wear headscarves and sometimes the full veil. The Fatih area on the European side, and Uskudar on the Asian side are known for their more conservative Islamic populations.

Kurds

Istanbul has a significant population of Kurds, who originate from southeastern Turkey. They are not formally recognized as a minority population and no data are collected on their numbers. For the most part, Kurds are heavily integrated into everyday life of the city. There are some extremist Kurds who demand an independent Kurdish state. Separatists have occasionally carried out violent attacks against targets in Istanbul.

Women in Istanbul

Dilek Cengon is 18 and lives in the Bakirkoy district of Istanbul. She works as the personal assistant to a TV director on one of Turkish television's best known soap operas. "It's a great job," says Dilek, "but I will need to learn more about producing TV programs and speak better English if I am going to make a career in television.

"I love Istanbul—it's where most of my family and good friends live. It's fun to grow up here as a girl in the Muslim community because there is a lot of freedom for women to do what they want here in Istanbul. I like to go to parties and dance clubs, sometimes with brothers and other members of my family, but mostly with my good friends. Istanbul has everything you could need and I am able to enjoy a wide range of activities. My favorite sports are swimming and volleyball and I also enjoy tae kwon do and Latin dancing."

▲ A young woman tries on sunglasses in a street market. Istanbul's women benefit from many of the same freedoms enjoyed by men and women elsewhere in Europe.

Istanbul's Greeks

Since the 1950s, the Greek population of Istanbul has declined enormously and they today number only around 2,000, compared to around 200,000 in 1920. Many Greeks left Istanbul (and Turkey) after September 1955 following events in Cyprus, where Greek Cypriot nationalists were attacking British and Turkish Cypriots for control of the island. In Istanbul gangs of Turkish nationalists reacted by rampaging through the Greek areas of the city, destroying Greek businesses, schools, churches, and homes. Greek citizens living in Istanbul were expelled by the government, leaving only those Istanbul Greeks who held Turkish citizenship.

Today Greek-Turkish relations are much better and Istanbul welcomes thousands of tourists from Greece who come to visit the Orthodox Patriarchate in Istanbul (the headquarters of the Orthodox Church). Some Greeks in Istanbul still complain of unfair treatment by Turks because of their ethnicity, but violence is now rare. Two Greek newspapers are still published in Istanbul, and there are several Greek secondary schools.

▼ Children from the Turkish-Greek community. Istanbul's Greek community has shrunk by around 90 percent since the 1920s, when Greece and Turkey went to war.

The Jewish community

Jews have been in Istanbul since Byzantine times, but large numbers came in the 15th century to escape religious persecution in Spain. Today's 20,000 Istanbul Jews have a strong sense of identity, with their own primary school and secondary school, hospital, and weekly newspaper. Historically the Jewish community was clustered around Galata and Balat, but many have now moved to newer districts farther out of the city. Istanbul's Jews live peacefully alongside the majority Muslim community, but they have occasionally been the target of violent attacks by Islamic extremists. In 1986 gunmen (thought to be Palestinians) killed 22 worshippers at the Neve Shalom synagogue. The same synagogue was partially destroyed in 2003 by one of two car bombs at Istanbul synagogues that killed 20 people and injured close to 300.

Armenians

Istanbul's Armenian community dates back to at least 1453, when they were welcomed to settle in the city by its new conqueror Mehmet II (see page 14). Kumkapi, on the southern shores of the Golden Horn, is the center of the community today. Like the Jewish community, the Armenians have a strong identity, with their own schools, community centers, and churches.

greater freedom to live and work in Istanbul, further adding to its diversity.

Tolerance has long been a feature of Istanbul, so the city is well placed to absorb and celebrate its growing diversity. Recent years have seen examples of intolerance and episodes of violence, but these are largely associated with extremist groups determined to destabilize the Turkish state. The majority of Istanbul's people do not share such extreme views and many take great pride in the openness and hospitality that their city offers people.

▲ St. Antoine's, the principal Roman Catholic (Latin rite) church in Istanbul.

Global diversity

Globalization and the ease with which people can now travel are today enhancing the diversity of Istanbul's population. People from Russia, Ukraine, China, Korea, Somalia, Iran, and Iraq are among the many recent migrants to arrive in Istanbul. In some cases these people are fleeing persecution in their own countries, but in others they are merely seeking a better quality of life and improved job opportunities. With Turkey seeking to join the EU, the attractiveness of Istanbul to such economic migrants can only increase. Membership in the EU would also allow residents of other EU countries

▲ Though still dominated by Turks, Istanbul's population is increasingly diverse and is likely to become more so as globalization allows foreign nationals to live and work more freely in the city.

Living in the city

The lifestyle of Istanbul's population is influenced by its ethnic and religious diversity, and is also characterized by wide-ranging socioeconomic variations. The city's elite enjoy top restaurants and designer stores to rival those of any European capital, and yet not far away, Istanbul's homeless take shelter beneath underpasses, in parks, or along the waterfront. Access to housing, education, and employment as well as social connections are all vital in determining the way people live.

▲ Like any global city, Istanbul has some homeless people who find makeshift shelter such as here, in an archway of the old city wall.

"Paris of the East"

During the height of the Ottoman era Istanbul was frequently known as the Paris of the East in reference to its splendor and wealth. These qualities are still evident today and for the wealthy and privileged, Istanbul offers a quality of life equal to that of the elite in New York, London, or indeed, Paris. As the economic center of Turkey (see page 30), Istanbul naturally concentrates wealth. While this helps fuel demand in areas such as services and retail, it can also causes difficulties. One such difficulty is the price of property in Istanbul, which has seen sharp increases since 2000 and is today beyond the means of even some middle class professional households. For those who can afford it, however, there are plenty of options from luxurious waterside villas to desirable city center apartments.

▼ The Akmerkez shopping center is one of the best in Europe, complete with expensive designer stores—a sign of the growing affluent middle class that enjoys a high standard of living.

Gated communities

A recent addition to lifestyle choice in Istanbul is the emergence of American-style "gated communities" that began to appear on the city outskirts around 1995. These housing developments promise a better quality of life than that offered in other parts of the city. They offer safety, peace, a lack of traffic congestion and pollution, and amenities such as child care, social clubs, and sport and health facilities. Though the quality of life is good, such communities are criticized by some urban planners for their negative effect on people's sense of belonging and identity. Residents become more associated with their own community than with the wider city, while those living "beyond the gates" become resentful of the unattainable lifestyle within. This is said to damage notions of shared citizenship and enhance inequalities. For the elite of Istanbul the gated communities have proved popular and further developments are planned.

Gecekondu

At the opposite end of the spectrum from gated communities are Istanbul's *gecekondu* (see page 19). A typical *gecekondu* house begins as a small single-story building often made of light materials salvaged from building sites. Inside there will be two or three rooms (the kitchen and bathroom are often one) and outside there is a toilet and perhaps a small yard for growing food or keeping poultry. Over time *gecekondu* houses develop to meet new demands. Further stories may be added, some sections rebuilt with better materials, or the yard built over to house a growing family or newly arrived relatives.

▲ Many *gecekondu* houses start out as simple structures similar to this, but most have been replaced by low-rise apartments today.

When *gecekondu* first appeared in the 1940s the city authorities attempted to clear them, but the workers they housed were needed to fill low-paying jobs in Istanbul's industrial and service sectors. Realizing that preventing them was impossible (and politically unpopular), the authorities instead began to improve conditions in the *gecekondus*. Roads and facilities for water, sanitation, and electricity were put in place and loans made available for improving buildings. In return, residents would pay a local tax toward the upkeep of these services. Today, many *gecekondu* are low-rise apartments (*apartkondu*) built by property developers and rented out. Land is often acquired for such developments by promising existing occupants an apartment or two in return for moving out.

Education

Istanbul's education system mirrors that of Turkey as a whole, providing for a good basic education. The majority of people over 15 are literate, though the rate is higher for men than for women, at 94 and 78 percent respectively for the period 2000–2004. The system is less successful at the secondary and tertiary levels, with around a quarter of pupils not enrolling in secondary school.

▲ Low rise apartments are the norm in Istanbul today, many of them built by property developers on land that initially comprised *gecekondu*.

▲ Istanbul has a mix of state-run and privately funded education that ensures a good level of basic education. This primary school is in Uskudar.

Schooling begins around the age of seven and is compulsory for eight years. Turkish is the main language of instruction, but some international or community schools (such as the Jewish schools) use a second language. Istanbul has nearly 1,500 primary schools, a little over 600 secondary schools, and 20 universities. The University of the Bosporus is the most prestigious center of learning in the city, while Istanbul University is one of the largest, with an academic staff of over 6,000 and around 68,000 students.

▶ Istanbul University is one of the largest in the city and in Turkey.

CASE STUDY

University student

Emre Cogal is a student at Istanbul University where he is studying Shipping Engineering. "Istanbul is a great place to be a student," says Emre, "but it can be very difficult too. The city has everything a student needs—great museums, art galleries, movie theaters, and concert venues to see international bands. On the down side, Istanbul is expensive and most of the museums and galleries are too expensive for a student to visit very often. The biggest cost though is housing—this is particularly expensive.

"Nevertheless Istanbul is still a great place to live. Each part of the city is unique and distinctive. There is so much variety that it never gets boring. I hope to finalize my studies in Italy and after that I would like to get a job here in Istanbul. The city is noisy and dirty and the traffic is terrible, but there is no other place I would like to live. I know in 20 years' time Istanbul will be even bigger but I think it will still be able to retain its rich cultural and social mix."

▲ This haze hanging over the city is caused by polluted air, one of the major environmental challenges for Istanbul.

Health

Many of the health problems in Istanbul are related to poverty and quality of life measures. Breathing disorders and eye complaints, for example, are common as a result of the air pollution and smog that affect the city. Health care is provided by around 200 hospitals, with a mixture of state run and private facilities. Private hospitals tend to be smaller and have higher standards of service than state hospitals, but all charge for their services. For those on lower incomes and without private or state-funded medical insurance this can be a major barrier and poor people are known to suffer symptoms for a long time before seeking treatment as a way to try and save the fees. Many people hope to avoid hospital fees by visiting a pharmacy (there are close to 4,000 in Istanbul) for advice and medicinal drugs instead of a hospital. Not all pharmacists have qualified staff, however, so this can often be a false economy.

Climate

Istanbul's climate is close to the typical Mediterranean climate but with much colder and wetter winters. Its summers can be very hot, with temperatures reaching 90°F (32°C) or more in July and August. Winters, by contrast, are much colder, with an average temperature in December to March of around 45°F (7°C), but sub-zero temperatures not uncommon. Strong north winds are common in the winter, and it is not unusual for Istanbul to experience snow. Precipitation falls mainly during the winter and averages around 4 inches (100 mm) a month between November and

▼ People enjoy a fine autumn day near the Haghia Sophia. Besides a short cold winter, Istanbul enjoys pleasant temperatures and plenty of sunshine for much of the year.

February. May to August is the driest period, with average precipitation of 1.5 inches (less than 40 mm) per month. Climate only becomes an issue in Istanbul during extremely hot days in the summer months and very cold periods during winter. The strong winds of winter can also cause disruption, leading to ferry cancellations across the Bosporus Strait.

▲ Strong winds can disrupt ferry services across the Bosporus. The wind and extreme temperatures are the only major climate hazards for Istanbul.

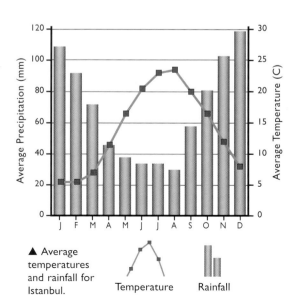

▲ Average temperatures and rainfall for Istanbul.

Temperature   Rainfall

Crime and safety

By world standards Istanbul is a relatively safe and low-crime city; however, in common with many other global cities the incidence of crime is slowly rising. Much of the petty crime (robberies and pickpocketing) in Istanbul targets tourists, and Istanbul has its own tourist police to patrol busy tourist districts and provide security for its lucrative tourist industry. There is some evidence of an increase in organized gang-related crime in Istanbul.

Several extremist groups pose a continuing threat of terrorist attacks in Istanbul and have attacked targets in the city before. Some of these groups are related to Kurdish separatist movements fighting for an independent Kurdish state in southeastern Turkey. Others belong to extreme Islamic groups, some with international links to al-Qaeda and others. As in any major city, the authorities in Istanbul have taken measures to try to minimize the risk of such attacks, but terrorists are always a risk.

▲ Istanbul has its own tourism police to provide security for thousands of tourists who visit the city each year.

The Istanbul economy

Though losing its status as capital in 1923, Istanbul has always remained the economic heart of Turkey. The income generated by businesses in Istanbul accounts for almost a quarter of Turkey's national income, and Istanbul's tax contribution composes 40 percent of the annual state budget. Despite this significance Istanbul's economy is in need of considerable investment and expansion if it is to meet the needs of its fast-growing population and compete in increasingly global markets.

▲ Istanbul dominates the Turkish economy and is its most attractive city for most international investors.

Industrial growth

Istanbul's rapid population growth is largely attributable to its industrial expansion since the 1950s and the demand for jobs that this created. People from rural areas all over Turkey poured into the city to take up paid work in factories that sprang up in the suburbs. The majority of Istanbul's industries are manufacturing rather than heavy industries. They include the manufacture of textiles, metal goods, paper, footwear, flour, food products, cigarettes, automotive components, glass, pottery, and

▼ Most of the industry in Istanbul is today located on the outskirts of the city center such as this food processing plant.

leather goods. Petrochemicals, shipbuilding, vehicle production, and cement works are among the heavier industries present in the Istanbul area. In total Istanbul accounts for half of the largest industrial companies located in Turkey and for around 40 percent of the country's total industrial output.

A successful industrial sector in recent years has been the automotive industry. Turkey has become an attractive location for vehicle manufacturers because of its lower production costs and skilled workforce. The Istanbul region is the focus of this growing industry, with international companies such as Ford, Opel, Fiat, Hyundai, Honda, Daimler-Chrysler, and Renault all investing locally.

Location, location

A main attraction of Istanbul to international investors is its strategic location between the markets of Europe and Asia. Companies locating in Istanbul have easy road, rail, sea, and air access to a vast market of customers on both continents, not to mention the growing market in Turkey itself.

CASE STUDY

Textile industry

Fatih Altunyurt works for Ismen, a large textile company based in Istanbul. "Turkey is one of the world's most important textile producing countries," explains Fatih, "and there are many companies like ours in Istanbul. We specialize in upholstery for chairs and sofas, but others produce clothes or bulk fabric. Istanbul grew around industries like textiles, but this has led to problems of overcrowding and

pollution. The government is now encouraging companies like ours to move outside the city by giving us loans for relocation and reduced rates on services, such as water. They want to make Istanbul a cleaner, more pleasant place to live. The new factories will also provide employment in areas where housing is more affordable for workers. We are taking advantage of this opportunity and relocating our factories from Istanbul to about 60 miles outside the city. I will stay in the city at head office—Istanbul is still the business center of Turkey."

▲ An international textile trade fair in Istanbul.

The strategic advantages of Istanbul to manufacturing industries are obvious, but Istanbul is also becoming increasingly popular with financial and other service sector industries. The headquarters of virtually all the private banks based in Turkey are in Istanbul, for example, and the telecommunications, real estate, and computer software industries are also growing rapidly. The municipal authorities consider these commercial business–oriented industries essential to developing Istanbul's position in the global economy.

▼ Modern office towers are coming to dominate parts of the city skyline as Istanbul's service industries expand rapidly.

Skills for the future

A large proportion of Istanbul's workforce is semiskilled or unskilled and has only completed the elementary stages of education. Such levels of skill are well suited to low-paid jobs in the manufacturing sector but do not attract the higher value service sector employers that the city is eager to entice. Completion of secondary schooling is considered the bare minimum for employment in service sector jobs and in many cases a degree or other form of higher education is required. The city authorities offer scholarships to students studying for higher-level degrees at a university as part of its policy to raise the skill profile of Istanbul's workforce. Learning English is also considered central to this policy, because it is considered the global language of commerce. The most sought-after schools in Istanbul are those that teach English, giving their pupils an added advantage when they enter the workplace.

▲ Learning new skills based around computers and information technology is considered essential to Istanbul's future economy. Internet cafés provide cheap access for people to practice their skills.

As industrial and manufacturing processes become more reliant on automated technology and less dependent on labor, the need for Istanbul to develop a new economy built around the service sector will become even more important. Not only will such measures help to reduce unemployment (which is as high as 25 percent in some of the poorer *gecekondu* districts), but the higher-level earnings will boost taxes for the city, enabling it to make much needed investment in local amenities, infrastructure, and the environment (see page 56).

CASE STUDY

Learning English

"My name is Sareb Mustafa and I am a teacher at Kalem Egitim Primary School in Uskudar on the Asian side of the city. Kalem Egitim is a private school and I am the English teacher here, working with students in the first two years of their primary schooling. English is considered an extremely important subject in Turkey—it is the language of global business and in a city like Istanbul that is very important. In fact, many parents will ask about how good the English department is at a school before deciding to send their children there. Parents encourage their children to learn English from an early age. Even though the children I teach here are seven years old or younger, many will have started learning English in their nursery school before they arrive here to start primary school."

▲ A shoe shiner at work—one of the many jobs to be seen in Istanbul's informal economy.

The informal economy

An increasing number of women are working in professions such as health care and education, as well as for local government and in the expanding retail and tourist industries. Women also form a major element of Istanbul's informal economy—an unregulated economic sector in which workers do not pay taxes and are unprotected by labor and safety laws. The informal economy in Turkey is officially said to make up around 20 percent of economic activity, but many put the figure much higher. Researchers in the textile industry, for example, state that for every job in the formal textile industry,

there are a further 10 in the informal sector. The textile industry (see page 31) is particularly suited to the informal sector and in Istanbul is organized as piecework, whereby workers (virtually all of them women) are paid for each item they complete. This allows women to fit work around other activities such as caring for the family and maintaining the home. It also means they can work from home. The downside for women is that they have no protection against low pay or unsafe working conditions and are unable to join any form of union.

▲ These women cooking Turkish bread in Eminonu are typical of the informal sector economy in Istanbul, providing essential services but lacking any formal status.

In 2003 wages for women completing piecework were around 50–75 percent of the official minimum wage. The Working Group on Turkish Women Homeworkers claims that the garment industry (75 percent based in Istanbul) relies on informal sector women for 60 percent of its labor. Since 1994 the group has been lobbying to improve conditions and in 2001 established the first cooperative for women textile workers in the Avcilar district of Istanbul. This brings home-working women together to collectively market their products to small retailers, thereby getting a better price and improving their working conditions.

▲ Spices are one of the commodities that were once stored and traded in the *hans* of Istanbul.

The *hans* of Istanbul

An unusual feature of Istanbul's economy are its *hans*. A *han* is a building of several stories that normally surrounds a courtyard. They were built during the Ottoman era to stable and shelter overland traders and their goods. Each *han* was known by a particular trade (honey, cloth, spices, fur, and so on) or by the nationality of its occupants. Istanbul's *hans* are no longer used for shelter and warehousing, but for a mixture of small-scale economic activities. Many house artisans producing fine crafts, while others have been converted into small cafés or shops. Though by no means significant in terms of economic output, the continuing existence of *hans* provides a physical reminder of Istanbul's long history as an important center of international trade and commerce.

Managing Istanbul

The continual growth of Istanbul makes managing the city a complex and challenging task. The current limits of the Istanbul Metropolitan Municipality (IMM) were set in 1984 and cover a total area of 707 square miles, of which 376 square miles is on the European side and the remaining 331 square miles on the Asian side. Across this area the IMM is responsible for a range of services including transportation, waste collection, health care, public spaces, and cultural services.

▶ One of Istanbul's municipal buildings.

Local government

IMM is headed by a mayor who is elected by the public to a term of office lasting five years. In the most recent elections of 2004, Dr. Kadir Topbas, an architect and former mayor of Beyoglu district, became mayor. Mayor Topbas was elected with a strong vision for restoring Istanbul to its glory as a world city and has introduced new planning controls to protect its natural and cultural heritage.

The IMM is further divided into 32 District Municipalities (DM), each with its own elected mayor and council. The mayor of each DM, together with a fifth of the council members, sits on the metropolitan council, which is chaired by the citywide mayor and is the city's main decision-making body. A metropolitan executive committee also has the power to make decisions independently of the metropolitan council. This consists of the mayor, the secretary general of the metropolitan government, and the heads of municipal departments including urban planning and development, public works, finance, legal affairs, and personnel and administration.

The city corporations

Many of the services provided by IMM are delivered by metropolitan companies, of which there were 18 in 2006. Hamidiye Spring Water Corporation, for example, delivers water to neighborhoods not connected to the water mains as well as bottling water for sale across the city and beyond. Kiptas is the public housing corporation, formed in 1987 to provide high quality affordable housing across the city. Their projects have seen more than 20,000 houses constructed between 1995 and 2005. As new challenges emerge new companies have been formed such as Agac, the Istanbul Tree and Landscape Corporation, created in 1998 to help green the city and provide open spaces in an increasingly congested city.

▶ Municipal workers plant one of the gardens being developed to green the city.

The People's Bread

Halk Ekmek is the People's Bread Corporation of Istanbul, one of the city corporations providing services to the people of Istanbul. It began baking bread for the city in 1978 and today its factories produce around 1.6 million bread products every day, sold through some 1,500 bread kiosks and other retail outlets. Alpaslan Yuru works in Gaziosmanpasa, one of several factories run by Halk Ekmek. "Bread is an essential food and should be available to all," he explains. "That is what we do here, bake high quality bread at a reasonable price so that everyone can afford it. At the moment we are baking only 50,000 loaves a day at this plant because it is Ramadan and people are fasting during the day. Normally we would bake 600,000 loaves every day. One of our newest markets is for organic bread. At the moment we bake around 5,000 organic loaves daily, but demand is growing fast."

Earthquake hazard

Istanbul is located in a region of active fault lines and is at considerable risk from earthquakes. The last major earthquakes to affect the city were in 1999, when two quakes of over 7 on the Richter scale struck the Marmara region of Turkey near Istanbul, killing more than 18,000 people. Those earthquakes were centered along the northern Anatolia fault line, which also passes through Istanbul, and each one struck farther west, toward Istanbul. Experts working with IMM predict that there is a 62 percent chance of a major earthquake striking Istanbul before 2030. Predictions for Istanbul, based on an earthquake of magnitude 7.5, are very worrying. Up to 80,000 people would be killed in such an earthquake, with a further 200,000 hospitalized and around 500,000 left homeless. The physical cost would also be enormous, with up to 50,000 buildings destroyed and a further 250,000 suffering moderate to extensive damage. The total rebuilding cost of buildings alone has been estimated at US$11 billion.

The IMM is working to minimize the earthquake risk by ordering the rebuilding of some of the most at-risk structures—many of them poorly built residential buildings. Regulation of building standards has historically been slack in Istanbul and the construction industry has often been associated with corruption. Major new projects are closely monitored, however, and undergo intensive design and testing to withstand an earthquake of magnitude 9 on the Richter scale. Such safety is especially important for recent underground transportation projects such as the metro (subway) and the Marmaray tunnel (see page 41), which could be carrying hundreds of thousands of passengers at the time of any future earthquake.

▼ Many of the buildings in Istanbul are of a dubious construction standard and at serious risk of damage or collapse in the event of a major earthquake.

Joining the European Union

Fikret Gersoy is 35 years old and is building a career in tourism. "At the moment I work as a night receptionist at a tourist hotel in Sultanahmet," explains Fikret. "I work at night because it allows me to earn money but continue my studies during the day. I am studying at a university to train for working in the tourism and travel industry. This is already very important for Istanbul and Turkey and will be even more important if we join the European Union [EU]. I think joining the EU would have major economic benefits for Turkey, and especially Istanbul. It would make it even easier for people to come here and boost trade. It would also make it easier for Turkish people to travel to Europe on vacation or to work. At the moment we have to apply for a visa every time we want to go abroad. We have to fill out long application forms and explain to our employers everything about our trip. The whole process takes a long time and is expensive. If we were part of the EU, Turkish people would be much freer to travel and Istanbul would benefit from closer links with other big cities in Europe like Paris, Berlin, and London."

Transportation for Istanbul

Istanbul's position makes it a natural transportation hub, a factor central to its foundation, growth, and development. It is the meeting point of the European and Asian rail networks, a key overland road link, a major ocean port, and a growing center for air travel. Within the city, transportation faces the challenges of blending an ancient layout with the demands of a modern economy and growing population. Innovative approaches to public transportation and an ambitious vision are helping to build sustainable solutions, but these are challenged by growing private car ownership and increasing traffic.

International port

The Bosporus is as important as ever to international transportation and is one of the busiest shipping routes in the world. Over the period 1994–2002 an average of 132 vessels navigated the Bosporus every day—over 48,000 in a typical year. Around 60 percent of shipping is passing traffic and does not dock in Istanbul, but there are extensive port facilities on both the European and Asian sides of Istanbul, mostly located on the Sea of Marmara. In

▲ As air travel, particularly within Europe, becomes ever cheaper, Ataturk International Airport is of increasing importance as a major transportation hub for both Istanbul and Turkey.

recent years these have undergone extensive upgrading and expansion to handle an increase in Turkish port traffic. The Marport container terminals on the European side saw volume increase by 68 percent between 2002 and 2005, for example. In total the ports of Istanbul handle around 45 percent of Turkey's exports and approximately 40 percent of its import trade.

◄ A container ship in port. Istanbul's ports have had to improve their efficiency and upgrade their facilities to keep pace with the growing demand in traffic, particularly for containerized goods.

Bridging the continents

Istanbul has two major bridges that cross the Bosporus to connect the European and Asian continents. The first, the Bosporus Bridge, was completed in 1973 and the second, Fatih Sultan Mehmet Bridge, was completed in 1988. Both bridges are for road traffic only and between them carry an average of 330,000 vehicles daily in each direction. A third bridge is currently being discussed to cope with the increased volume of road traffic in Istanbul.

Another new crossing to bridge the continents is a rail tunnel to pass underneath the Bosporus in an earthquake-proof tube (see page 38). The Marmaray tunnel was started in 2004 and is scheduled for completion by 2010 as part of a 47-mile east-west rail link connecting the Asian and European sides of Istanbul. The new rail link will be used for passenger commuter trains and for freight. It is predicted that the tunnel could handle up to 12 times the daily passenger capacity of either of the existing bridges, with an eventual daily flow of some 1.7 million passenger journeys per day by 2025.

▼ The Bosporus Bridge is one of two bridges that provide the main crossing points between the European and Asian sides of the city.

The Marmaray tunnel is expected to dramatically increase the use of public transportation for crossing the Bosporus because it will reduce travel times significantly. By 2025 when the new system is at full capacity it is expected to save over 100,000 hours of travel time (equivalent to 11.4 years!) every day. The share of people using rail (including metro) for their journeys is expected to increase from less than 4 percent in 1997 to almost 28 percent when the tunnel opens. This would give Istanbul the highest rail share of any global city after Tokyo and New York.

▲ Passengers on board the metro. Istanbul is seeking to massively boost rail travel in the city by 2025.

Transcontinental transportation

The Marmaray tunnel will not only ease traffic within Istanbul, but also provide a seamless link for rail freight between the markets of Europe and Asia. At present most freight transported between the two continents is brought by sea or by the Trans-Siberian Railroad through Russia. Plans were announced in 2004 to build a new rail link from China to Europe that will connect to the European rail network through Istanbul. In 2004 Turkey also signed a treaty with 27 other Asian nations to build a Trans-Asian Highway that will link 32 countries via an enormous road network connecting Istanbul to Tokyo. Both plans are now being developed by the countries involved and are designed to boost east-west trade. The rail route, for example, would reduce the journey time for goods from China to western Europe from around 50 days by sea to around eight days. Both the rail and road links will substantially boost Istanbul's role in global trade if they are completed.

▼ Rail freight being transported across the Bosporus by ferry. The Marmaray tunnel will remove the need for this time consuming and costly activity.

City congestion

Traveling within Istanbul is often subject to major traffic congestion. The city covers just 1 percent of the land area of Turkey, but is crammed to bursting with a quarter of the country's motor vehicles. Around 90 percent of all journeys in Istanbul are by

▲ Traveling by road in Istanbul can involve major traffic delays, especially on the access roads to the main Bosporus crossing points.

road and the number of vehicles on the city streets is estimated to be growing by 500 every day! Traffic is so heavy that during peak times the average road speed can be as little as 5 miles per hour and long waits are common, especially to access the crossings over the Bosporus. The problem is not just congestion and the lost business time caused by traffic. Pollution is a major problem because many vehicles use lower grade fuels and there are poorer emission controls than elsewhere in Europe.

Public transportation

Istanbul's public transportation has developed haphazardly over the years and includes buses, metro (subway), streetcars, ferries, and local shared minibuses known as *dolmus* (meaning "filled up" in Turkish). Buses are operated by the municipal government and private operators and run regular and cheap services in most parts of the city between around 6:30 a.m. and 11:30 p.m. The bus service is supplemented by the *dolmus*—private minibuses that depart when they are full, dropping and collecting passengers on the route. They follow many of the same routes as buses but also serve other parts of the city and run after the buses have stopped.

▼ Passengers disembark from a *dolmus*. These minibuses are a vital part of Istanbul's public transportation network.

Istanbul has several rail-based forms of public transportation, including streetcars, metro, light metro (*hafif* metro), and an urban rail line on both the Asian and European coasts that will be joined by the Marmaray tunnel (see page 41). Most of these systems have only been in place since 1989 (the metro only opened in September 2000) and are ongoing projects with new extensions under construction or in planning. The goal is to transfer people off the roads and onto public transportation by making the systems attractive and efficient to users (see box).

Surrounded as it is by water, Istanbul's ferries and water taxis are alternatives that have become central to the city's transportation policy. A new city corporation, Ido, was set up in 1987 to operate services and reduce congestion. By 2004, Ido was operating 26 vessels,

▲ Ferries run regularly across the Bosporus carrying both vehicles and passengers. The fleet has been gradually expanded since the early 1990s.

with a further nine due to enter service during 2006–07. These vessels carried 12 million passengers and 960,000 cars in 2004, representing a substantial reduction in road traffic.

▲ Istanbul's streetcars are modern and efficient and run along dedicated tracks to avoid the congestion of the city roads.

Sustainable transportation

The Istanbul Electricity, Tram and Tunnel (IETT) is responsible for running the Tunnel (a small funicular railroad), the trams (streetcars), metro and light metro, and city buses. In 2006 IETT and other public transportation agencies were put under a single umbrella organization to make managing the growing transportation problems easier.

Zeki Gumus, a manager at IETT, explains: "Transportation is one of our biggest challenges, and daily congestion is a real problem. In addition to hundreds of thousands of private cars there are 18,000 yellow taxis in the city center alone. Millions already use public transportation daily—not just the trams and funicular, but also the new metro and the ferries that link Istanbul across the Bosporus. We must encourage even greater use of public transportation.

▲ Passengers use the *Akbil* (inset) to pass through entry gates and access the streetcar service.

"One of the big successes of recent years is the introduction of the *Akbil*. This is small metal disc that can be refilled with credit like a phone card. *Akbil* is accepted on around 91 percent of public transportation vehicles in Istanbul and makes getting around quick and easy. We are now working on the '2023 Plan'—2023 is the centenary of the foundation of the Turkish Republic and we are using it as a target date to further improve the sustainability of Istanbul's transportation network. The metro network will be extended from 75 miles of track to 186 miles and will be better integrated with the tram system. We will also introduce incentives to reduce road traffic such as congestion charging. This is all intended to make the Istanbul of the future a more efficient and sustainable city."

Culture, leisure, and tourism

Istanbul has been a center of culture for centuries and is often referred to as a melting pot where different cultures meet and fuse. Where once this meeting of cultures was largely East meets West, Asia meets Europe, the influences on Istanbul and its people are increasingly global in their reach.

▶ A group of young Muslim women enjoy a fast-food snack. The recent popularity of Western fast food outlets is a visible sign of the increasing global influence on local culture.

A careful balance

In 2005 workers excavating the European side of the Marmaray tunnel entrance unearthed important ruins that typify the challenge facing Istanbul. The rail link and tunnel are vital to the Istanbul of the 21st century, but the discovery of a fourth-century port, complete with whole boats and portions of the ancient city walls, is one of the most important archeological finds in a city rich in history. The archeologists have significant powers and have been able to freeze construction while they continue to excavate the site. The city authorities are impatient to resume the tunnel construction for its planned completion date of 2010, but they may be forced to re-route the tunnel if the finds prove to be significant and worthy of permanent preservation. Similar conflicts between the past and future of the city are common and regularly raise questions of Istanbul's culture.

◀ The historic streetcar line that runs between Taksim Square and the Tunnel was reinstated in the early 1990s and is an example of how Istanbul is managing to modernize while retaining elements of its distinctive heritage.

Architecture and museums

Istanbul is endowed with impressive architecture, much of which incorporates stunning works of art such as mosaics and decorated tiles. Topkapi Palace, Haghia Sophia, and the Blue Mosque are arguably the most famous of these architectural wonders, but there are many others including the Galata Tower and Dolmabahce Palace. Its history means Istanbul has a wealth of museums including the Archaeology Museum, the Museum of Turkish and Islamic Art, and the Ataturk Museum. It also has some more unusual museums including a cartoon museum, rug museum, and even a UFO museum exploring the paranormal and extraterrestrial.

▲ Tourists visiting Topkapi Palace, one of the many architectural wonders of Istanbul well known for its ornate tiled artworks.

CASE STUDY

Cultural riches

Dwight Frindt is on vacation in Istanbul with his daughter Noel. "We live in California and came here because we have a great interest in Islamic art and culture," says Dwight. "Istanbul is a wonderful place, a beautiful city with some of the most spectacular mosques. For me the Blue Mosque in Sultanahmet is one of the great architectural achievements of the world. Its ornate dome, decorated pillars, and graceful minarets are masterpieces in their own right. And this is just one of many attractions the city has to offer. Istanbul is also a great place to get a feeling for the history of Europe and Asia. Over the last 2,000 years the city has been influenced by many of the great religions. In the Haghia Sophia, for example, there are beautiful Christian mosaics right alongside Islamic art. There are so many different communities living side by side here, including Orthodox Greeks and Jewish people. I think it is interesting and educational to experience a city that has such a remarkable mix of cultures and to see how they all get along with each other."

Performing arts

The performing arts of Istanbul represent a wide range of tastes, from classical through to contemporary and popular. They also cover a range of styles from both eastern and western traditions and are becoming increasingly diverse as the city continues to globalize. Theater, films, ballet, dance, opera, and art are all represented at numerous venues across the city and there are important art, film, and theater festivals held annually that attract an international audience. Music is particularly vibrant in Istanbul and ranges from folk and classical through rock, jazz, and world music to European pop. On the streets the most common form of music you are likely to encounter has come to be called "Arabesque"—an electronic fusion of Turkish folk music and Asian and Arabic sounds and rhythms. Arabesque stars outsell all other forms of music in Istanbul and leading stars attract an almost religious following.

Mevlevi prayer dancers

The Mevlevi (whirling dervishes) are followers of a Sufi (mystical) form of Islam, who express their faith by whirling ecstatically, accompanied by traditional music. The dervish orders were outlawed in 1925, because they were seen as reactionary forces opposed to modernizing Turkey. Later the Mevlevi were allowed to re-form as a cultural organization, and they now perform their traditional *sema* (whirling) for tourists, although the performers remain dedicated to the Sufi way set out by their 13th century founder, Mevlana Celaleddin Rumi.

Belly dancing

Belly dancing is often part of a typical tourist itinerary to Istanbul, but is actually Egyptian in origin. Nevertheless, belly dancing, known locally as *oryantal* (oriental), has grown in popularity since it was first brought to Turkey (probably in the early 20th century). In 2003 the Turkish winner of the Eurovision Song Contest, Sertap Erener, gave belly dancing a newfound audience and helped remove its sometimes unsavory reputation.

▼ A belly dancer performs for tourists at the Galata Tower.

▲ Sufi dervishes spin in worship at the Mevlevi Tekkesi, the famous Sufi lodge in Istanbul.

Sports

Soccer is by far the lead spectator sport in Istanbul (and Turkey) and the city hosts the three leading teams in the country—Galatasaray, Besiktas, and Fenerbahce. All have competed in European competitions, with Galatasaray winning the UEFA cup in 2000 and Besiktas reaching the quarterfinals in the 2003 competition. Rivalry between the clubs is intense and the fans are known as some of the noisiest in world soccer. There are even leaders to coordinate the chanting of fans and maximize the intimidation of their opponents, especially when hosting overseas teams. Basketball is the other main spectator sport and local teams are growing in status within the European leagues.

Participant sports are limited by space, leisure time, and money. For the wealthy there are limited sports facilities, but otherwise participant sports are limited to informal soccer games, jogging, and cycling along the Bosporus. Skating and skateboarding have a following among sections of the youth of the city.

▲ Galatasaray players celebrate after winning the UEFA cup in 2000 after beating the British team Arsenal 4-1.

▲ Backgammon is a popular game in Istanbul, often played by men frequenting one of the city's *kiraathane*—coffee or tea houses.

Leisure time

Many people in Istanbul work long hours in order to make a living and spend several hours traveling to and from work from the outskirts of the city where housing is more affordable. This is particularly true of the city's lower earning population. Because of this leisure time is often associated with family and friends and revolves around eating together or (for men) enjoying time at a local *kiraathane*—coffee or tea house. Modern cafés and bars are emerging as an alternative meeting place in the trendier parts of the city frequented by tourists and students and bringing a more European feel to the city. One different feature, however, is the growing popularity of the traditional *nargile*. This is a water pipe for smoking heavily flavored tobacco that is filtered through water. The *nargile* can be smoked alone, but is often a social activity shared by a group of friends. The resurgence in popularity of the *nargile* is an example of how Istanbul is modernizing but retaining strong cultural elements that help the city carve its own identity.

Tourism

Istanbul is one of the premier tourist destinations in Turkey and the eastern Mediterranean, popular with the cruise-ship industry as well as with tourists who arrive by air. It also attracts considerable visitor numbers who come to the city for business and international conventions. Lower European air fares and an increase in the number of international routes connecting to Istanbul all helped to boost tourism in the city during the 1990s, but growth since then has been less steady. The al-Qaeda terrorist attacks on New York in 2001 shook the confidence of tourism worldwide and visitor numbers fell dramatically due to fears of attacks against tourists. Istanbul, as a predominately Muslim city, suffered a particularly severe slump in numbers and only began to show strong recovery by the end of 2005. In that year visitors to Turkey, many of whom

◀ A family enjoys one of the many pavement cafés and restaurants to have opened in Istanbul over recent years.

prioritize a visit to Istanbul, increased by around 22 percent compared with 2004, giving Turkey a record high of over 20 million visitors. Visitors come from all over the world, but the majority come from Germany, Bulgaria, Iran, Greece, and Russia.

▲ Tourists take time out to check their guide book and decide where to visit next. Tourism is becoming a key industry in Istanbul.

CASE STUDY

Tourist numbers

Mustafa Cesur sells carpets in his store in Sultanahmet. The bulk of his customers are tourists, but as Mustafa explains, relying on tourists can be a risky business. "Like many places we were badly affected by a downturn in tourism after the 9/11 terrorist attacks on the World Trade Center in New York. We have struggled to rebuild confidence in Istanbul as somewhere safe to visit, and I and other salesmen have struggled to make ends meet. The first year we felt things were slowly improving was 2005, and we are all hoping that visitor numbers will continue improving. But now we have a new fear of bird flu and I am worried that might scare some tourists away—I hope not."

The Istanbul environment

The rapid expansion of Istanbul over the past 50 years has seen vast stretches of land surrounding the city paved over for housing, industry, or infrastructure projects. In turn these developments have placed strain on water and energy supplies and led to growing levels of pollution and waste generation. Recent economic prosperity has only served to further aggravate matters: Trends include rising consumption levels and a daily increase in vehicle numbers.

▲ The decorative stonework of the Egyptian Obelisk in the Hippodrome area of Sultanahmet has been damaged by air pollution—one of Istanbul's greatest environmental problems.

Air pollution

On an everyday basis, poor air quality has long been the most serious environmental problem in Istanbul. An ever-growing number of vehicles churn out a daily cloud of pollutants to which industries, power stations, and domestic energy sources all add their mix. These all combine to cause regular smog problems that create poor visibility and health issues including eye, nose, and throat irritation, and respiratory illnesses. The municipal government has implemented numerous initiatives to reduce air pollution such as banning low-grade coal and introducing measures to convert power generation to cleaner natural gas. Igdas was established in 1986 as a city corporation to oversee the conversion of the city to cleaner-burning natural gas. By 1995 Igdas had around 300,000 subscribers but sulfur dioxide levels were still around 250 micrograms per cubic meter—well above the World Health Organization (WHO) guidance levels of 150 micrograms per cubic meter. By 1997 levels had fallen to 115 micrograms per cubic meter and have not surpassed WHO levels since. The number of subscribers to Igdas services had increased to 3.1 million by mid-2006 and the gas network now reaches almost every part of the city.

Other forms of air pollution such as lead particulates are being tackled by phasing out unleaded gasoline and converting many of the city's taxis to run on methane gas rather than gasoline. IMM is also encouraging industries to relocate away from central Istanbul in order to reduce industrial emissions. Investment in public transportation initiatives such as the Marmaray tunnel and subway extension are designed to shift people away from dependence on road traffic.

▶ Investment in a new subway system for the city is a key strategy to reducing traffic levels in Istanbul and the consequent air pollution.

Waste management

Istanbul's residents and industries produce vast quantities of waste, presenting a considerable challenge for the authorities. Up until 1953 the majority of this was dumped in the sea, but as the city grew, informal garbage dumps were formed across Istanbul. The need for new housing meant many of these dumps were close to housing, or indeed new housing was built on top of dumped trash. None of the dumps was properly managed and toxins escaped into the air and water with ease. The garbage dumps presented significant health and environmental hazards. In 1993 an unstable dump in the Umraniye Hekimbasi area collapsed, causing some 386,000 tons of trash to fall 1,640 feet onto the Pinarbasi neighborhood. Hundreds of homes were engulfed and 32 people were killed.

▲ Trash collection in Istanbul is managed at a local level by each District Municipality and delivered to centralized waste facilities.

A new city waste corporation, Istac, was established in 1994 to improve management of the city's waste. Istac immediately closed the hazardous waste sites and opened two new sanitary landfill sites, one on each side of the Bosporus, and five garbage transfer stations. The transfer stations handle around 1,500 trucks per day, collecting locally generated waste and compressing it for transfer to the main landfill sites. In total this system was handling around 11,000 tons of solid waste every day by 2005.

Istac hopes to increase rates of recycling in future years to further improve the management of the city's waste. A new composting facility, for example, reclaims around 770 tons of organic waste on a daily basis and converts it into useable compost. In addition to Istac's activities, there are numerous informal recycling ventures in Istanbul for everything from paper to plastics.

Below is a breakdown of the typical composition of Istanbul's solid waste:

Organic material	45.0 %
Paper	15.5 %
Ash	15.0 %
Plastic	9.5 %
Textile	5.6 %
Ceramics and bricks	4.4 %
Glass	3.8 %
Metal	1.2 %

▼ A man collects plastic bottles for recycling from a trash bin in Eminonu.

Green space

One of the main environmental initiatives in Istanbul since the early 1990s has been the greening and beautification of the city. Open spaces are important for residents to escape the confines of overcrowded residential areas and provide a "living lung" that contributes to reductions in air pollution. In 1996 IMM launched a campaign to green the city called "100,000 Trees for Istanbul." This target was easily surpassed and the targets were ambitiously increased so that by 1999 some 2.5 million trees had been planted in the city. In 1998 the Istanbul Tree and Landscape Corporation was formed by IMM to continue this work. It has established a tree nursery capable of producing over

2.5 million trees a year and worked to improve existing green space in the city. For the future there are plans to link the Sea of Marmara and the Black Sea with a green corridor of open space for its recreation and air cleansing properties.

▶ Green space in one of the riverside parks near Yedikule is used by local people for a family picnic.

CASE STUDY

Threats to the Bosporus

"My name is Yesim Aslan and I'm an activist for Greenpeace in Istanbul. There are many threats to the city's environment, but one of the biggest concerns is condition of the Bosporus Strait and the increase in hazardous materials that are carried through the city on a daily basis. The waters of the Bosporus are much more polluted than they used to be, and few people would swim in them today. Ships passing through the Bosporus are polluting the water with fuel and oil, and of course the great worry is that there could one day be a major spill. Besides shipping the sewage waste of millions of people living in Istanbul flows, largely untreated, into the Bosporus, not to mention industrial wastes! A new hazard is the increase in the number of old ships being dismantled in the docks. These ships usually contain quantities of highly toxic materials, which can be released into the Bosporus when they are broken up for salvage."

The Istanbul of tomorrow

Istanbul may be a city famous for its history, but it is also a city with a strong vision of its future. Buoyed by recent economic growth and the recent (December 2005) commencement of Turkey's negotiations to join the EU, Istanbul's current mayor, Kadir Topbas, wants Istanbul to take its place alongside New York, Tokyo, and London as one of the most important cities in the world.

▶ Another new skyscraper emerges on the Istanbul skyline, right next to one of the new metro (subway) stations. This modern urban scene is very much part of the vision that Istanbul's authorities have for its future.

Centenary goals

Turkey will celebrate 100 years since the foundation of the republic in 2023 and this landmark date is being used by IMM to galvanize efforts for improving Istanbul and making it a city fit for the next 100 years. Improving the city's ailing transportation infrastructure is key to these goals. Transportation is key to any city, but particularly one so divided by its geography as Istanbul. The Marmaray tunnel, a cornerstone of Istanbul's transportation policy, is a reminder that Istanbul is a city built on history, and there is a need to preserve this unique culture and identity.

European capital of culture

In 2006, Istanbul was elected by the European Union to be the European Capital of Culture in 2010. The award was welcomed as proof of Istanbul's growing status in Europe and the world and will bring welcome investment from the EU as Istanbul enacts plans to attract 10 million tourists to the city for 2010. Historical buildings will be restored, archeological sites uncovered, and areas of unplanned concrete development pulled down to beautify the city and give it back to the people.

▶ These wooden buildings are among the last such structures in Istanbul. The conservation and restoration of such buildings will be a major part of Istanbul's preparations for being European Capital of Culture in 2010.

Bold visions

The plans being implemented to build the Istanbul of tomorrow are based around some bold visions, and the IMM recognizes that they may not always be popular. If they work as planned, however, Istanbul is set to once again become a city not just of global importance, but also of global admiration. It will again take its place as one of the most important cities in the world. At a crucial time in fragile east-west relations, its continuing role as the meeting place of cultures and continents may have much from which we can learn.

CASE STUDY

Nilufer Kuyab

Nilufer Kuyab has lived in Istanbul for most of her life. "The city has changed dramatically over the last 30 years," she explains. "It has expanded hugely and absorbed many small villages and towns along the Bosporus. Place names ending in 'koy' were once villages—such as Ortakoy, which I remember as a small fishing village on the Bosporus, a few miles from the city walls. Today, it is surrounded by the city, but like many neighborhoods still manages to retain some of its identity. Interestingly it was the place where President George Bush of the United States chose to give one of his most famous speeches on the Iraq War, with the backdrop of a mosque and the

huge suspension bridge linking Asia and Europe, East and West. Istanbul has always been symbolic of this link and is just as important today."

Glossary

al-Qaeda An international terrorist organization that follows an extremist form of Islam and has conducted acts of violence against individuals and nations that contradict its views.

Catholic Church A Christian church that recognizes the Pope as its head and is administered from the Vatican City within Rome, Italy.

cosmopolitan Composed of or containing people from many different cultural or ethnic backgrounds. Often used to describe a multicultural place and especially a city.

crusaders Christian armies that were active in the area of present day Turkey and much of the Middle East during the 11th to 14th centuries in order to repel Muslim armies and reclaim Palestine for Christian rule.

economic migrants People who move to an area in order to seek employment or otherwise benefit from the economy of that area.

ethnicity A person's or group's ethnic identity or distinctiveness, for example Turkish, Greek, or Kurdish.

European Union (EU) An economic and political union of 25 European nations that cooperate on issues such as trade, international relations, the environment, and social justice.

Eurovision Song Contest An annual contest held between European nations to find the best new song of the year. Famous winners include Abba. Turkey won the contest in 2003.

fault line A geological feature in the Earth's crust marking the boundary between plates and subject to sudden movements in the form of earthquakes.

fiefdom A territory controlled by a feudal lord, who is normally a powerful individual, or by a powerful group.

globalization The process by which the people and countries of the world are becoming ever more interdependent and connected. This is evident in areas such as trade, travel, communications, and the sharing of languages and culture.

Islam The religion of Muslims, based upon the teachings of Muhammad during the seventh century. It is second only to Christianity in the number of worldwide believers.

mega city A city with over 10 million inhabitants. Istanbul is the only mega city in Europe.

Orthodox Church A Christian church that originated during the Byzantine Empire and acknowledges the Patriarch of Constantinople as primate (principal leader) rather than the Pope.

particulates Small particles of dust and or chemicals that become suspended in the atmosphere as a result of natural or human activities. They form a main component of urban air pollution and can lead to smog.

precipitation Rain, snow, or other moisture that forms in the atmosphere and falls to the ground.

Richter scale A logarithmic scale that measures the force of an earthquake. It uses a scale of 1 to 10, with a higher number indicating a more powerful quake.

smog A mixture of atmospheric moisture (fog) and particulates, such as those from smoke or exhaust fumes, that form a polluting blanket damaging to health.

Sufism (the Sufi sect) A mystical form of Islam that is best known for its followers expressing their faith by whirling ecstatically to enter a transcendental state that brings them closer to God.

sustainable development Development that improves the lives and well-being of people today without degrading or depleting the natural environment to the detriment of future generations.

unions Labor organizations that are formed by workers to negotiate better working conditions or pay for their members.

urbanization The process by which a country's population becomes concentrated in towns and cities.

visas Legal documents issued by a government and recognized by other governments to allow international travel of individuals between nations. Many countries require an individual to present a visa before granting them access.

Further information

Web sites

BBC News Country Profile: Turkey
http://news.bbc.co.uk/1/hi/world/europe
/country_profiles/1022222.stm
The BBC News Web page for information
about Turkey. Includes information about
the country and links to recent news items
such as the process to join the EU.

Istanbul.com
http://english.istanbul.com
A city portal providing background
information, and detail of specific places.
The "Exploring Istanbul" section is very
useful.

Istanbul Metropolitan Municipality (IMM)
http://www.ibb.gov.tr/en-US/AnaSayfa/
The official web site of the IMM, with
information about the mayor and the
organization and structure of the city.
Good for up to date news of key events.

Lonely Planet WorldGuide: Istanbul
http://www.lonelyplanet.com/worldguide
/destinations/europe/turkey/istanbul/
A site provided by the Lonely Planet travel
guides that gives some good basic
introductory material about Istanbul and
planning a visit.

Marmaray.com
http://www.marmaray.com/
A site that allows you to find out all about
the Marmaray project to link the European
and Asian sides of Istanbul by a tunnel
under the Bosporus.

Virtual Istanbul
http://www.virtualistanbul.com/index.html
A site that provides information about the
art, history, and museums of Istanbul.

Books

Barber, Nicola. *Istanbul*. Great Cities of the
World series. Milwaukee: World Almanac
Library, 2005. A photo-filled introduction to
the history, landmarks, culture, people, and
economy of the city.

Eyewitness Travel Guides: Istanbul. New York:
Dorling Kindersley, 2003. A travel guide
featuring brief historical notes and
numerous full-color photographs.

Freely, John. *Istanbul: The Imperial City*. New
York: Viking, 1996. A biographic history of
the city from its origins to the modern day.
One of the most popular history books
about the city.

Keyder, Caglar. *Istanbul: Between the Global
and the Local*. Lanham, Md.: Rowman &
Littlefield. A scholarly study of globalization
in Istanbul, one of the oldest world cities.

Pamuk, Orhan. *Istanbul: Memories and the
City*. New York: Knopf, 2005. One of
Turkey's best-known novelists writes about
growing up in Istanbul and the changes he
has witnessed in the city and its people.

Pavlovic, Zoran. *Turkey*. Modern World
Nations series. Philadelphia: Chelsea
House, 2004. Illustrated reference for
in-depth study of Turkey, for readers grades
6 to 12.

Index